In
My
Skin

By
Deborah Ramos

To El Elyon Elohim, male and female, in the "let Us make them in Our image" GOD, to Jesus, to Spirit and ultimately, to me and walking in my skin…finally.

<u>In My Skin</u>
<u>Table Of Contents</u>

1.   ...I Am
2.   A Change In The Air
3.   Be It So
4.   Canvas
5.   Divine
6.   Faith
7.   Happy Birthday To Me
8.   I Am Again
9.   I Am NOT
10.   I Am The Love Of A Greater Design
11.   In My Place
12.   Lest We Forget
13.   Let's Make It Rain
14.   Letting Go
15.   Love
16.   Oh My Child
17.   Overcoming
18.   Release
19.   Shoes
20.   Stand
21.   Storming
22.   They Call Me Magic Woman – for LadySpeech
      Sankofa
23.   This Is Me
24.   Traveling
25.   Tribute
26.   Unfettered
27.   Weep
28.   In My Universe

...I Am

Soften the breeze as I whisper my tongues in which I sing
The air quietly attunes itself to my spirit and I breathe a new
breath
I am
A divine daughter
I am
A holy lover
I am
A faithful sister
I am
Growing
And I am
Whole
And holy I am
Healed
Delivered from all evil
Because I am
Loved
And I am Loving Love
There is none other like you
There is none other like me
Yet we are brothers and sisters
Fathers and Mothers
Uniquely One yet never the same
I offer to you my willing hand

To offer you some truth
But to your truth I will no longer bend
I am Divinely made
By the hands of GOD
And I have the breath
Of Woman
And I Am

A Change In The Air

There is a change coming
And I hear
People...get ready
There is a new sun a-rising
With a moon now a-singing
The cawing crow
The whistling raven
Sounding their call of Come Those Who Hear The Sound
Is it for all?
We know not
But if we dare listen
But if we dare try
Love will not deny
What our souls have long longed for
Yes, there is a change a-coming...
Signs and wonders to follow
Meeting a new day and a new tomorrow.

Find the face of the new moon now a-singing
It's all just a beginning.

Be It So

Be it so
Never it be naught
To find me at
The side of LOVE
I cannot fight
The knowing sight
That fills my eyes
My heart too wise
To not let it go
With no more heart's woes
I stand and lay
Down at the feet
Beside LOVE I rest
My form to sleep
And I shall be
Shall be it so
I won't stand down guard
From what I know
No disagrees
Nor apologies
My beacon shines

Onto the light of Destiny
And I shall be
Shall be it so
No false bindings
Only find what is true
Be it so
Never it be naught
To find me at
The side of LOVE

Canvas

I paint with my words
Onto a canvas paved out onto the fabrics of the gods
Woven by the Creator of the universe
Knowing that my design is like none other
I understand what I once lacked
What my song delivers is what my heart echoes
Into caverns of ancient landmarks I dare not move
They are sacred
They are holy
I am honored to be among the many who seek yet the few who achieve
The Finding
What has been found, you may ask?
Yet I hesitate to answer
See, there are mysteries to be sought out
To tell just because one is asked may be the answer of a fool

And I have learned that holy things are to be tucked into sacred
pockets within my spirit,
Nurtured within my soul,
Protected and harnessed to its fullest potential within my form as its
power does what it will
Sometimes the words are not to be said
Not to be painted
And I have learned
Not all are meant to be delivered from their chains for they alone
Have the key
And sometimes
Yes, sometimes
You are not to save your enemies
For with a whisper they may entrap your soul if you are not aware
With their words of kindness they hide their hate and malice and
their forked tongues
Yet I paint chosen words with Love
For He knows
And She is knowing
That as sons and daughters of painted and spoken words
We are ministers of the alchemy that transmutes from unseen to seen
We are the power to raise the dead,
To save the soul,
To protect the innocent , defend the widow and comfort the weary
and broken
We are the fire of the Divine
I paint with my words
Onto this canvas…
And I declare
That we have only just
Begun.

Divine

I stand, a being divine
What does this mean as woman inclined
To nurture, to birth?
To create, to faith stir?
Here is what I know
If in words alone...
In the begin Spirit breathed
Word was spoken and there was
And now there is what eternally was
So I am Divine who knows The Vine
I am designed to walk free of chains
That which conquered sin and Death
Frees to be the life in me and I am in service to be divinely me
Words sinking as Love into me
I now awaken
What to be...

Faith

I listen
Do not think I do not hear
The call of Your Spirit is coming in clear
The reception removes all doubt and chases away fear
Enter in Love, it is You that I declare to be real in a world and realm where
Faith, Hope and You, Love are but a dim gong of a distant cymbal
When You desire, O Great Love, to be heard in the hearts of all
You, Love, with so many names…
I listen
And I dare respond
I run to you,

Not only in the night hours when darkness comes to hide me from demons that once had me bound for come, they do
They try to remind me that I had once been their toy, their boon, their bounty
But Love came and conquered each and every one
You teach me, Love, that in the darkness You are still present, Loving me
Fighting on my behalf, teaching me how to wield my sword and use my shield
My song
My word
My dance…my laughter!
How once they had been stolen and yes, once I had given them away to fools and thieves
But LOVE, how You loved on me and love on me still…
So when the morn comes and the mourning ends and joy begins to flow as if each fruit of my past labors are being bourn
My toes begin to tap
I begin to hum
And a certain battle hymn starts to rise because faith is…
Faith is dancing within my core, within my being
And I see You inviting me to dance with You
To war against fiends that would steal life with my pen and my song
So Love, come faith with me as I begin this day
And let's make it Ours
Come divine with me, for You Are and because You Are
I am and I Am more than I once was
I Am all I Am made to be and I Am wholly unashamed to belong to You.
Therein lies my Faith
So Day
You may begin.

Happy Birthday To Me

Silence

Quiet

Learning to be alone

Without leaving a barren hole

I am whole, this I know

I have been loved

I know GOD

I know Love and Love knows me

I will not put a label on such

And there will be no label put on me

If I choose solitude over a crowd of people just one more time

I will choose worship yet again in my own fashion

I hold to no sin

I hold to no paradigm or diagnoses for they are to me

One in the same

I will travel to distant places

Different realms where with Love there are no disgraces

No shames with their old embraces

It is my time to seek forth new dialogues and conversations

New ways to love and manners of my many faces

I am me

I am always She without the We's

Happy birthday to me!

I Am Again

Good day to you, I pray
And pray for you, I do,
Every day
I always have, and for that some ills have befallen me
But now I say "had" for such ills no longer grip me
Yet I have something to say as I pursue righteousness each moment,
you see
Years have passed, temporal time yet sometimes it's yesterday to me
And to truly get passed words and deeds said and "innocently"
slandered towards me
I must release these bones that sometimes crush and break my skin
Impaling me outward from within and try to bind my soul to speak
me as a sin
So please
Don't judge my reality
Mock my curiosities
Actually, because of those same curiosities
My reality may be realities
Because I dare to travel in and through plentitudes of uncharted
realms and territories
Yes, you may call me crazy
I have been labeled certifiable many a time before
But those with the labels never asked
Only judged
Never questioned my path
Only deigned to box me in
Yet I must give thanks and praise these days
I have learned to sometimes saunter and sometimes simply graze
Into lands and dimensions that no drug or hallucinogen cannot
fathom to create
Because this is how I was created and made
And I am not ashamed
It has given me this writ
This vision
This gift
I may not be meeting your standards of faith

I may be in your mind a loon, a boon for the devil
Evil, a lost cause to the Kingdom of God, insane
But I am again
Loved
Loved by the One you somehow deny me
Yet you pray for healing of my mind
And I pray for the opening of your eyes
Jesus loves me
This I know
For not only does the Bible but He tells me so
So I know Love and no, you can shame me not
I won't hide Love from a hungry, searching soul
Simply because of your judgmental rot
Yet I know your heart means well
Intentions are good maybe even pure
But your meting out of words and actions only cause seekers to run
And sometimes declare to be done with the One we seek to share
And then the seekers respond in pain as if the One has never for them been there
But see, for me
I know He
Loves me
And I am
Again
Unafraid
To be
His Beloved.

I Am NOT

Here is the law of my land
With the pen in my hand
I write with the script what I declare…
See, I will not to rhyme right now
There is too much to write right now
Too much wrong to make it right

With the write of my pen…
And I realize this, you see,
That it is all in me that I seek

But the question is not what I am
I could write what I know and believe myself to be
But that is not today's offering
It is time for the sacrifice,
For the offering to the wild goddess within me that
Reaches
Deep into the Divine that promises no scatterings
And I will begin there

I Am NOT scattered…
Though if I were to yield to yesterdays and yesterdays and
yesterdays…
I would succumb to the lava of molten Death which would burn me
to ash
I would yield to others…yet not all but some
Yet not some but maybe one
Who's hate and resentment would try to be as if she had power over
my soul
But see? I Am NOT scattered
In my mind I know me
I know the me's I had become and still carry and they are virtuous
Seeking wholeness in what had once been seeking lawlessness…
Not in the spiritual sense but in the longing for freedom
The longing for wild and for the stretching of wings and arms and
legs that didn't mean
Spreading for man to take of me
Because taken I had been
So many times my mind cannot receive the memory…

Alas…
I go too far back

I Am NOT a monster…
I am beautiful, simply put.
Punto.

Sometimes denying the mirror is welcoming my soul wonder.
Embracing the woman of wonder which comes from a deep core
ALL THE WAY out to hair I wish I hadn't relaxed
See, I miss my curls
I want to love my form, this body that I spoke love to
Just this morn'
She deserves to be wanted by me
She was given Queenship and desires to be seen that way
To be honored and cherished by the spirit being who dwells within
That would be me
Words of old…
Wow, I am done fighting
My armor is of a kind that is impenetrable by others except my own
kind of weapons
I wound myself by the declaration that I am faulty
Broken
Ugly
Fat
Unwanted
Unworthy
All the while pushing love away
Extrapolating from all of my own bruisings that I am nothing
But my body knows that I AM something beyond what others see
Because I don't see what others see
I struggle to see beyond old inconsistencies
How can I say I live true, love pure, if to this beautiful Divine
daughter of GOD
Of Mother and Father filled with Spirit
I deny her worth and her identity
As beauty?
As Aphrodite walking,
Venus waiting…?
See, I see and read into mythologies and lore what isn't there
I am waiting for Eros not to be clipped by his own arrow to not be in
love with a Psyche who was struck by arrow of love false
I want the real thing
Yet I have me.
I have beauty, inside and out.
I AM no monster.

So I will declare these I AM NOT's
That are just a few and ask that what I declare cover those that want
me to be to them true.
And I receive the I AM's so much more than I did earlier on
Because I ask of me
To lovingly
Receive
And to press on.

I Am The Love Of A Greater Design

I am the Love of a greater Design
I am the perfected piece of the grand puzzle crafted by the
Divine
Love is my crafting tool and the mirror that sometime doth
blind, I find
That my heart deems to cause trouble because purity is not vain
in its course
And the tears my heart bleeds soul into the page of my spirit so
loud the world can't help but hear it
"Keep your way," it screams,
"Watch out for the wisdom of the ravens and crows masqued in
the dark"
And I laugh in fear for ravens and crows are mystery
enshrouded and I,
Since laughter hides my discomfort, walk on through veiled
forests of mystic realms

16

Wander into places where my form is mine as my eyes see in my dreams
And I recollect that I am beautiful as I am now
Full and lush and warm
Beautiful and powerful, bountiful and plentiful, full of love and body to hold
I am the Love of a greater Design
I know me and I know what is Mine
Nothing and no one dare question or take that which is my kind
For Love has told me time and time again
What my soul has been screaming out for eons and times past
I will go forth and not cry out for the past to be reborn unless in plain sight
Miracles and magic manifest every curve and every perfected and imperfect line
I am the Love of a greater Design.

In My Place

I choose to be single
Singular and one
All to myself
To my one-ness
To my wholeness
To my all-in-one-ness

Needing

Wanting

Just me, myself and I

And I am proud of meself, darn skippy

Hear thee my word!

I declare it!

I proclaim it!

I lay it on the line that I chalk on the cement

That I draw on ancient sands of forsaken, forbidden time

I fold my love in runic rhyme all for myself

Been too busy loving on outer divine

That I forget that I too am same divine

That there is no woman, no female such as me

That I am more than…

That I am lioness…

Raven…

An inspiration to myself as it should be.

I should look at the mirror and flip my own switch

Be that wondrous witch and kick each defying bitch to the curb

This is my world now

It's time I claim it

No more screeching night hags allowed to defame it

I am surrounded by the Power for Love and in Love I'll rename it

To This IS Me, I Don't Care Who She Be, I Am Me

Empowering my soul

Facing pained memories of old so that I will walk aware

And yes, I dare

To stare

Down betrayers and traitors and liars and falsi-fiers

Can no longer burn me with your hellfires

Up to me to consume what I will with my firebrands

My love is more than can be handled so I'll handle my love myself

I know who I am and it's just a matter of time before I know what I don't know now

Tomorrow is a new day and I choose to embrace it as my own

No longer can you deface me, I embrace me

So goodbye, screaming nightwench

My own thirst I will quench

I am second to none

Better write that down, son

I am still daughter of El Elyon

I am still bride of the Son

There is nothing else for you to attempt to make undone

I am full of knowing

No longer will I be showing you what heart is on my sleeve

I call you out and demand your leave

I'll stand not down but face to your face

My ire is up and all of me wants to put you in your place

But if I do, it'll just be a waste

Of my time and I will keep a wickedly, bewitchedly divine pace

I've already forgotten you, of you I've lost my taste

Here's the case: I take back my grace

I lend no more my womanly lace

Could speak curse but would rather not leave a trace

Of me for you to attempt to erase

I am just filling up my bones

Picking up each five stones

Knowing I got a pair of cajones

My spirit hears your moans

I care to let you go to the void with knowing crones

And see what the future brings

What manner of men and kings

For this warrioress that springs
Out of the ashes this phoenix sings…

Lest We Forget

How many times will towers fall,
Will beneath terror children crawl?

In how many ways will we die
Before to GOD's heaven will we fly?

When will suffering and pain cease to be
When it's our choice to stop the rain?

Can we choose to change the season?
Will in our hearts truly keep the Reason?

Love is our Bounty
Love is our Fuel and Force
Love is our Healer, our Balm,

Love our Protector, our Hero
Love our Fortress, our Teacher

When will we learn?
That even when bombs kill
And evil attempts to steal our foundation
That what speak
That what we do
Our thoughts
Our deeds
If founded and paid forward in Love
Can change
Can shift
Can lift the sorrows and the fear from stealing our souls' comfort
So Love
Give Love
Receive Love
Chains will fall
Strongholds will crumble
Wicked kingdoms will come tumbling down
Yet
Lest we forget
We can be that change
So be mindful
Not only in your head but in your heart
Not only in your heart but in your actions
Do good
Have mercy
Smile at a stranger
Love a sister
Forgive a brother
Times demand this
Love requires this
Your character may redeem a woman, a man
Lest we forget
We too could have been that fallen human
So in the midst of pain when fear desires to overwhelm
Know that Love has already won
And Love will win again.

Let's Make It Rain

To all my survivors and lovers of Life
I celebrate you
We, who live to embrace a life of victory
I glory in you
I dance for you
I stand in the gap for you
I rejoice for you
You are not alone
So come
It's about Love
It's about forgiveness, forsaking that which kept your face to the
ground
When it wasn't in a posture of prayer but of pain and sorrow
I am here for you
You may not me
You may never know my name
But you don't have to
I worship for you
The El Elyon Elohim
The Mother and the Father God of all gods
I walk with the Mediator who did the most amazing of things
Just for you
And I will not be ashamed to call on His Name
And Spirit…?
I breathe Wisdom and Discernment, Knowledge and Counsel and
Might in
Just for you
Just for me
And know this
You are never forgotten
And you are always
Always
Loved
So let's do something today

Let's make it rain
Rain grace and glory
Make our histories into stories that don't pain us still
Let's us forgive and release and dance into the newness of a new day
And remember that in making it rain
A new heaven and new earth will be
Treasures will unfold and eternity will ever be before thee
So let the rain
Fall.

Letting Go

(a sigh)
A sigh I release,
Realizing that this crossroads I have reached
Is one fated by GOD yet chosen by me
It is time
Time to let go
Not only to let go of ills and woes for I have done that over and over
again
They are not worth the time to repeat again – I've already shed that
skin
Let me go deeper this time…
Time…a word of whose essence I have lost
Me the survivor of some cruel game of coin toss
Once I would have written "victim" but that I am no longer
I have ceased claiming that label to be mine
It is time – that word again- time to reclaim what is inherently mine
A sound mind
A peaceful mind
One where delusionary visions have no place to find their fingers
twirling their lines
So much has been lost
Years gone from my memory
My body longing to remember what it is like to be freely me

And today I sigh
And I release
I release knowing that I am not a demoness
I am not possessed
There is no evil in me
Yet I let go of the wounded in me
Because freedom is needed
Clarity is called for
Truth as a banner I demand to be mine
I will pick up my sword and armor
Knowing my pen and my song
My dance and my simply being me…
Wow…this realization may simply astound my soul
Is it true?
If I am just me…?
Will the voices leave and intuition remain?
I choose not to wait another day
For release I embrace.

Love

Love
It is everywhere
It is in the She's, He's and Me's as well as in the We's of Life
It surpasses any distance set between Love's Other and Love Itself that is
Seemingly written in stone
It matters not so if a word is not said,
Love is there,
In the silence of a desert land or in the lush of a Paradise not made by
human hands
It is the culmination met in a newborn's gaze
It is in an embrace that you could only had dreamed of that comes to
surround
Love
Quietly rioting righteously

Leverage Over Vicious Enemies...yes, let's see that there are foes in this world

Foes decidedly against LOVE

But...

BUT Love conquers all, feeds all, covers all,

Rains on the stormy seas though rain isn't what the storm desires but a breaking to

Peace

Love

Coming over waves of energy so that no inertia sets in

Passing through realms and worlds and traditions

Seeking to change the most base of things into the most beautiful of imperfect perfections

Listen...

We with ears, unlike the rocks that are crying out for such Amazing, Infinite Love...

Put on your new garments

Lay down old armor that now only serves to cut you deep with memory passed

Wash your face

Comb your hair

Put on the purest of skins where no fig leaves are even a thought

The WAR IS OVER

And Love is left standing with arms wide open,

With no distance between starmet lovers who just know LOVE as LOVE is

No definition but

Wonderful

Counselor

Mighty

Peace

So much LOVE IS

In the Man

In the Woman
Know this and know it well
LOVE longs to take precedence over pain
Over insecurity that Love is for You, for ME, for Us
I have found in the lesson of the crossroads that one step in the right
direction is
An eternal mile towards the Essence of Love
And so Love...
We shall meet again for in Truth,
You never left me.

<u>Oh My Child</u>

Oh, my child
You of my dreams
You whom I love yet may never know
There are words I want to say,
Love I want to give and show
Sweet one, I shine with the glow of you
Though of my womb you will never be
Of my heart, I hold you close
I have imagined and heard your laugh, your giggle
Seen your hair and kissed your softest of soft cheeks
Yet I must say,
There is so much love inside of me
A mother's love that I have no child of my own to give to
All I have words to say is this:
If you have a dream to bear a child, you who read

Know that everything will turn out   to be in the end
As the Divine blesses
Love as if each child you come across has the breath of
The miracle of sonship and daughterhood.
We may not give to one of our blood
But we give to one of our Love.

Overcoming

It's done
I've been there, done that
An evolutionary kinda thing that had its chains, yes
That boggled and bound my mind, yes
But it is over, yes, and it is done
I am no longer there and that is no longer me
I am no longer afraid or terrified of whispers in the dark that
swirled inside my mind
Voices of terrified children, women and men who were me
when I couldn't be myself
Tell me my name no more
I know who I am even if I don't know my name at the moment
I am a child of the Most High, a daughter, a princess, a Queen
ever in the making
They call me Deborah and that is my name

I am no longer ashamed of being unable to remember the core of me
I am overcoming
Rather
I have
Overcome.

Release

....and in the yielding and surrendering to GOD, the tide turns and there is peace once again, finding that in the aloneness of me, myself and I, with the LORD I am not alone - I have a Friend, a Healer, a Provider who keeps this vivid mind company in the loud hours of the soul when quiet may seem too much to ask and pain seems too much to bear...He has given me sleep in the witching hour and covering when torment came to steal of me, sent healing to a body broken for naught and His Love has chosen to find me in this due season. I am no longer bereft of any good thing for His favor has begun to shower upon me as dew in the morning and the breeze of Spring's eve. I acknowledge Him and embrace Wisdom's call to be still and release each care for She knows Her child, Jesus said, and the Word that I read is anything but dead so I will rest upon Her bosom, listening to the heartbeat of the One created before the worlds were formed and cries out still on the city streets. It is of Her food that I will eat as I gladly release, yes, release the pains and sorrows of days that have tainted a moment this day and I say this, "the Bride says, Come"

Shoes

So I stand

In a pair of sneakers of a love I know well

I walk steady, knowing I am not alone

These shoes know strength and power

They carry Knowledge and Might

Discernment and Counsel, Wisdom and Fear of The LORD

Are part and parcel of their Hermetical wings

And I stand

Free and unashamed

Loved and loving

Breathing still and dancing wild

I am all that I am for this moment

Tomorrow has been promised

For I am not afraid of Death

It has been dealt it's own blow

By a Foe much bigger than itself

Love knows what Love is

I belong and I am sure

That makes all the difference in my reality

My perception shifts my conceived systems of manifested faith

And I walk

And I dance

And I laugh in the face of my past that wounded

And I remember laughing like a child

for I did laugh as a child even though there was pain

I was never truly alone in my soul

Alone was a lie

I believed in someone else's deranged pride

But now I believe in GOD and I believe

in my own

I deserve me

And LOVE?

Love is rightfully mine...
Just like these shoes.

Stand

I am standing

Glad to be firmly planted on solid ground

Glad to have found solace in the silence, the whisper and the
sound

Being the one I have sought for thinking I had been lost only to
be found

Once I had given my mind to shadows and myths of devils that
I don't doubt are real to this day

But I belong to the Divine, a daughter of I AM and on that
identity I stay and I remain

No one stole my soul for no one has the power to take me from
me

Granted I have been used and abused, beaten, raped and
tortured but no one can really take from me

Because if they did I would be in the ground six feet beneath

I wouldn't be the worshipper, the worshipped, the warrioress, the lover, the queen

I have learned to that in order to take my place in this plane I
must be bold and meekly state my peace

My piece of eternity stains others' mortality so my internal
immortal divine being authoritatively raises my pen as sword
and shield

My voice ringing throughout the realms of seeing

And I am grateful for new days and new nights of beginnings

For the shadows that once did haunt now yield hidden treasures
the wicked must yield to the righteous

For it isn't a sin to know if one lives rightly

It is wisdom

Clarity of living in the light of the sun and the covering of the
moon

So I stand this ground made of ancient song and writ

Knowing in my arms is where the LOVE that casts out all fears
and covers a multitude of sins may find rest and fit

And in this flow I have found a stream and a river

A sword, a buckler, with arrows and a quiver

Yet I don't seek war though I will not back down

I smile brazen if an enemy seeks my gaze for in the light if
LOVE

All must bow down

I know the wonder I am

I am Woman who surely does bear the weight of my crown

And I gladly stand

Gladly stand my ground.

Storming

There's a storm on the horizon
I can feel it a-comin' and I'm glad
Yes, I'm glad...
See, there are things that need to be scattered out of my way,
removed as debris
Ways of thought, unhealthy seeds
Habits and patterns that had choked me until deceived I had
yielded to my knees
I will pray bold prayers
Ask for greater things than these
That the Divine in me walk out in the woman in me no holds
barred
See, there's a storm on the horizon
She's coming near and I'm running to her, with my fist in the
sky
If a fight for my destiny has been fought, it has been won
As it rains on my scars that are full of wonder and beauty
I announce this - I am nebulous
I am a hurricane, blowing facets of fear and doubt and shame
effortlessly away from the land I have conquered,
The land shame had dared to claim for too long
It is mine
These words I paint with are mine to embody
For it is not with rage I rain
It is with Love I pour out on a dry and thirsty terrain
And I declare this land,
This once barren, abandoned land
Home.

They call me "magic woman"
They are right, for I am of such weavings
Tales I tell with the womb of Love within me
Divine cravings I fill with words that are ancient
Beyond measurings of Time for Consequence's sake
I can mold you
I can make you
I will not harm you unless you harm Love
And a child? You dare?
I dare aim and strike I will so do not dare harm what Love has
marked
But otherwise…yes, otherwise,
You will find Goddesswise Love flowing through every cell, every
pore
I know what seeps from me and the why's
I am proud of me and from whence I came
No matter the hurt and pain
I stand so I may serve you as I serve the Divine
My bliss I share so mine may grow and the Earth may heal
They call me "magic woman" and other things, some fake, some real
I am all things
Shame not one of them
Bitter no more unless it's chocolate and that is semi
I am feminine and I carry the masculine without doubt or fear
I know what you need and what you are
It's in the cards, written in the stars
But me,
You will never debase me or unwrite my story, my herstory
They call me "magic woman"
Nothing will lay me out
No one will make me lay down
The love I know only will grow as days pass and my hair grows
I am a child
I am a woman
I am a girl
I am a creator so don't defy me
Don't mess with my witchy soul

You don't want that, no sirree bob you don't
See, they call me "magic woman"
So pour on that sugar and toss that salt over your shoulder
You ain't known me before because I own my calling.
I am
A magic woman.

This Is Me

This is me

Hear me

Here I am

This is my refrain

I smile wide

Broken smile, it is mine

Here's my pride

My esteem inside

Stands arms at my side

I am of a unique kind

I have come from far and wide

To become the Me I am inside

Do swallow your pride

And see the One that I am

You disturbed my growth and took my say

I will not give you a moment or a time of day

I release from me what you gave as you took my gifts away

I yield to the GOD I love as you face Him

He's the One to ask The Forgive as He gives back the blessing
I admit The Fear gave you power over me but that power was
for a season
This is Me and I will live out the all of me
Your kind is gone and going and there is a Time and a Reason
I live and ask for Grace to be so that Jesus I am pleasing
This is Me
I am here
Hear me
It is my time to be restored and to go forward increasing
Yet as I do such and am the Desire of the Reason for the
Season
I breathe out hate and unforgiveness
I inhale God and Wisdom in female kind
I am Me
This is Me
I smile wide
Here is my pride
Broken smile coming to an end
I take in my hand the grace and power to mend
Restoration and renumeration to Love will have me as friend
And since you are gone
I can breathe again

Traveling

Been on the go
Unable to stay still
Afraid to remain after I've opened the door
That's been my m.o.
Don't want that no mo'
I long for home
To remain for awhile
Kick off my shoes and stay within my skin
Love within my beauty
Bask within my own love
Divinate between what is mine and what is…well, mine
I had given power to deceitful things
Found Love and had to watch Love find itself
Away
And tears came but I remained
Pain came but I remained
Madness fled because I remained
Sorrow knocks still at my door but I remain
I am no longer the broken doll left shattered on my bedroom
floor
That kind of broken in me doesn't exist anymore
I've done my time on Insanity Lane
I no longer have to revisit that pain
I've come home to me and to my Creator and don't need to
leave again
My soul travels to realms other than but my mind stays to mind

this plane

I am no longer afraid to step out of my home

I can open up my heart, choose to give it to the Adam who
gave his bone

That Adam I have the grace to choose

I have time to give yet no more time to lose

I don't have to worry about the offense of those I can afford to
offend

I speak a life to live with the curves and lines of this here pen

My goals are being created to live a new life once again

And who knows? I don't, right now, know what message to
send

All I know that in the dream that I live in

I am free to be me

And I'm traveling

Tribute

I am

Celebrating the function in my dysfunction

The creation and beauty in my malformation and defects

I am walking with pride alongside the broken child left
seemingly along the wayside

I understand sorrow was not the game plan mapped out for me

I weep no more for the little girl who thought she was a

blaspheme
Instead
I take her hand
And tell her this
"I am and you are
Beautiful
Able
Divinely human
Wonderfully made
Your scars are strategically placed on a face and body no one
dare erase
Others may try to emulate you,
Attempt to be like you and that is not a bad thing so you do not
have to fear any longer
So…
Little girl who is long become
Woman wonderfully made
It is okay at times to throw caution to the wind
Become wild like the ocean before a storm
You can always catch your calm
You have never meant to hurt anyone
And if you did, Love has always been in your eyes
So if to some you had to say some painful goodbyes
In order for you to walk with your head held high
It is time to embrace the living and inhale the skies
And live like tomorrow will never die
It is alright to walk on and to be healed
To let memories long lost perhaps remain lost

Yet treasures are meant to be sought…"
And so her hand I take
And I, the woman, promise to take each breath as a gift to give
back
I deserve this breath
I deserve this new day.
So tucked away in her garden in my heart
She no longer weeps for she understands and trusts
That
I AM.

Unfettered

Unfettered
Unencumbered
Unwilling to walk others' narrow road
I admit
I create!
And I'm lovely and strong and able
To live past old labels
To encounter the quintessential All That Is
I am magical and miracle-willing to do
I am fire, water, earth and air
I am blood, bone, special up to my hair
Yet most of these things,
I am this
Not to boast for I desire no hubris but esteem and strength
I am like you've never known

I am woman,
I am Love
I am unfettered to live out the ancient paths of my divine
heritage
Healing from wars that taught me
I don't have to fight.
I am Me.
And I am more than enough.

Weep

Up in the early morn
Eyes longing to sleep
There's a weep in my heart
For a broken wing longing to soar
I know it's a new season of change
An opportunity to rearrange
A time to weep
A time to mend
Holding my own breath
Waiting for GOD to breathe my way
And I'll wait the night out
No more screeching night owls
No more fowl wind spirits
Just songs of angels and Jesus singing over me
And this heart that is bruised by lesser things will give way to
lessons learned,
Love discovered in a past once of fire now tender flame
And I move on
Never forgetting to breathe.

In My Universe

In my universe
Children don't go hungry
There is no famine
There is no war
Poverty doesn't exist
In my universe.

In my universe
There are no genetically modified foods
There are no need for guns
There is no childhood cancer
No birth defects of any kind
In my universe.

In my universe
Every tree bears fruits
Every animal is not hunted
The ocean is clean and the forests grow
The birds, the bees, the glaciers are restored
In my universe.

In my universe
The seasons don't kill
Man knows their place
Their divinity is to nurture not destroy
Their humanity is to commune, not control
In my universe.

In my universe
Women are mothers
Men are fathers
Children play with one another
Death has been conquered and sin no more

In my universe.

In my universe
GOD is and Jesus reigns
The sons and daughters of GOD have awoken and responded to
the earth's call
Restoration and renewal and healing have come to one and all
Love is supreme and Satan is no more
In my universe.

In my universe
I am me
And you are you
Life is everlasting
Family and friends have come home after being departed for so
long
And heaven is on earth
In my universe.

www.ingramcontent.com/pod-product-compliance
Lightning Source LLC
Chambersburg PA
CBHW060634030426
42337CB00018B/3358